HOW

31-Day Journal to Practicing Self-care

By PAMELA LITTLE

MA. LCPC. ACS. LPC. ATR. RPT

Copyright

Cover Design: Richard A. Holder
RahCorp Visual Group

Editing: Leslie N.S

Author Photo Credit: Dfinney Photography

ACKNOWLEDGEMENTS

First, I would like to give thanks to the Lord and Savior of my life. The almighty God for his unconditional love, faithfulness, and hope. For my gifts, talents, and abilities placed inside of me.

Secondly, I would like to thank my friend, sister, and Coach Donna Barr for walking with me on my self-care journey to HOW YA LUV'N. Through this meaningful time, I learned to truly LUV myself while gaining clarity into my God given purpose. Donna consistently committed to coming alongside me that I might bring this process and support to many others.

Thirdly, I would like to thank my dearest friend of over 25 years, Joyce Daniels for the many mornings and nights of prayer and fellowship to birthing HOW YA LUV'N. She showed me what LUV'N yourself unconditionally really looks like.

Last but not least, to those friends and family members who provided brainstorming, listening, proofreading, and editing support … you know who you are! Thanks a million.

I pray this journal is a blessing to everyone that uses it and it benefits those around them. My best regards on your journey to HOW YA LUV'N!

HOW YA LUV'N

CONSISTENTLY COMMITTED TO CARING FOR YOUR SOUL!

This 31-day self-care journal is created as a special gift to those of us who recognize the importance of self-love. When we practice Agape' love we love according to scripture. Matthew 22:37-39 - Thy shalt love the Lord thy God with all thy heart, and with all thy soul, and with all thy mind. Thou shalt love thy neighbor as thyself. 1 John 4:8 - He that loveth not knoweth not God; for **God** is love.

This journal is intended to encourage all individuals to commit to truly loving yourself in order to give this precious gift to others. Galatians 5:14 says for all the law is fulfilled in one word, even in this; thou shall love thy neighbor as thyself. The three areas covered in this journal will support your growth in first loving yourself.

These practical tasks and activities supported me since 2006, when I had to stop and ask myself HOW YA LUV'N! I was broken and God took me on a journey of SELF-LOVE. I pray this journal will encourage you daily along your walk as well!

HOW YA LUV'N

H - HELPS US TO AWAKE AND ACKNOWLEDGE

O - OPENHEARTEDLY, AS GIVING

W - WITNESS TO

Y - YOUR GOD GIVEN

A - ABILITY TO

L - LOVE OURSELVES

U - UNCONDITIONALLY, WHICH IS

V - VITAL TO LEARNING

N - NEW PATHWAYS TO LOVING OTHERS

THE PERFECT GIFT

For God so loved the world, that he gave his only begotten Son, that whosoever believeth in him should not perish, but have everlasting life. John 3:16 KJV

LOVE is a gift! Will you receive it?

MIND

The Hebrew translate "mind" as "reins, kidneys, and spirit". Hosea 11:4, Proverbs 5:22.

Being mindful is a moment to moment awareness of thoughts, feelings, and sensations while renewing your mind in the present. Being mindful to renew your mind in Christ daily will connect you with the Creator to get clarity for life's purpose. Mindfulness will help you become focused so that a natural flow to create can emerge. This means a mind that is not ruled by fear, anxiety, depression, mood swings, and panic attacks.   But filled with peace, clear thinking, wisdom, creativity, good judgment, energy, and productivity.

2 Timothy 1:7 says for God has not given us a spirit of fear, but of power and of love and of a sound mind.

Romans 12:2   And be not conformed to this world: but be ye "transformed" by the renewing of your mind, that ye may prove what is that good, an acceptable, and perfect, will go God.

BODY

The Hebrew translate "body" as body, strength, bone, flesh. Sum of its part.

Mindfulness daily can support the process of healing your emotional, mental, and physical concerns leading to a more healthy and well balanced lifestyle. When this level of mindfulness is reached, your creative imagination gives over to what your hands, head, heart, and soul are doing. After which, the beginning process to deeply engage self is done.

1 Corinthians 6:19:20   What? know ye not that your body is the temple of the Holy Ghost which is in you, which ye have of God, and ye are not your own?   For ye are bought with a price: therefore glorify God in your body, and in your spirit, which are God's.

SPIRIT

The Hebrew translate "spirit" as wind, spirit, breeze, air, energy, life, person, intention, purpose, soul, and mind. (1:1 Ezekiel 37:9-10).

As you consistently commit to caring for your soul the connection between you and the creator are strengthened. You become more balanced and your lifestyle then can take on the direction in which it is purposed. Your spiritual eyes and ears are opened to the things God intends for your life.

Job 32:8 There is a spirit in man; and the inspiration of the Almighty giveth them understanding.

John 4:24 God is a spirit; and they that workshop him must worship Him in spirit and in truth.

Galatians 5:16 This I say then, Walk in the Spirit, and ye shall not fulfill the lust of the flesh.

Table of Contents

Day 1

Find a trail, park, or track and walk at least 30 minutes (preferably in the morning). As you are walking, immediately focus on clearing your mind. Then, remind yourself that you are there "to renew your mind" by meditating on things that are true, noble, just, pure, lovely, good report, virtue, and praiseworthy! Walking is one of the best methods as you are in "the nature" of things. You get to experience all 5 senses.

Practice deep breathing as often as possible during your walk. Acknowledge our thoughts and feelings without judgment. When I first started renewing my mind I was amazed at the challenge of staying focused. The difficulty of clearing my mind, but I was able to accomplish it when I became INTENTIONAL... fight for my mind!

Lesson learned: love myself, meditate on truth, relax, be intentional, and persevere!

Write at least 3 sentences describing your thoughts and feelings in the rectangle space below. Then create an image in the circle based on the adjectives described in your rectangle.

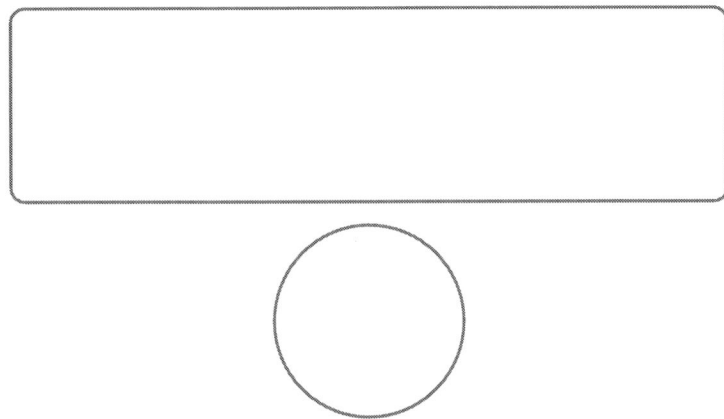

Day 2

Repeat day 1 in its entirety. Then integrate:

After walking to renew your mind, think of a scripture that resonates with your thoughts and feelings. Don't worry, a scripture might come up naturally. Commit to meditating on that scripture throughout the day and reading it before bed. As I walked I noticed that it was easy to repeat day 1. However, I noticed I was humming a hymn, then a rhythm in my steps. After which, I became more aware of the environment. The breeze, birds, traffic, heat, etc. The challenge was trying not to focus on any particular thought but acknowledging my hearts rhythm.

Lesson learned: love myself, keep purity of heart, relax, allow myself to become aware of the environment.

Write at least 3 sentences describing your thoughts and feelings in the rectangle space below. Then create an image in the circle based on the adjectives described in your rectangle.

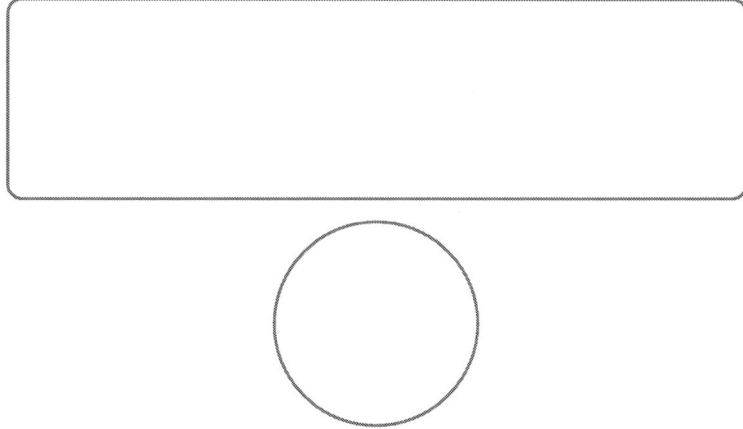

Day 3

Repeat day 1 - 2 in its entirety. Then integrate:

Practice complementing yourself through out the day (great job on attitude, being on time etc). As I walked repeating day 1-2, I noticed my thoughts around things I did and wanting my spirit to be free. I noticed my steps appeared faster as I would embrace the environment. I felt like I wanted to fly. The challenge was remaining focused on my breathing and steps to remain grounded.

Lesson learned: love myself by not judging, meditate on things lovely, relax, and count it all joy.

Write at least 3 sentences describing your thoughts and feelings in the rectangle space below. Then create an image in the circle based on the adjectives described in your rectangle.

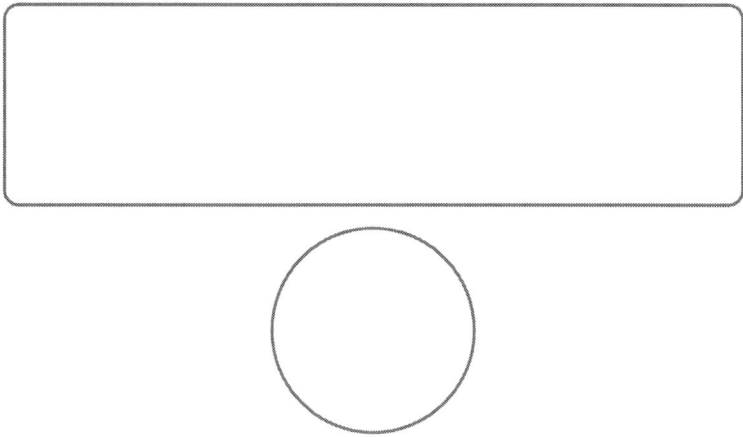

Day 4

Repeat day 1 - 3 in its entirety. Then integrate:

Practice communicating with yourself in a gentle tone and a humble attitude today. This will support a pathway for kindness and self control towards others. As I walked, I noticed my breathing and could hear my heart beat. I found my face relaxed, thoughts more focused on compassion for myself and my hips softened, making my steps more intentional. I was challenged with staying focused on breathing and controlling my emotions. I wanted to cry, but smiled at my sense of peace as the breeze blew in my hair. Seeing my tone and thoughts towards myself were sometimes strong.

Lesson learned: self-love, no judgment, meditate on things praiseworthy, relax, and let it go.

Write at least 3 sentences describing your thoughts and feelings in the rectangle space below. Then create an image in the circle based on the adjectives described in your rectangle.

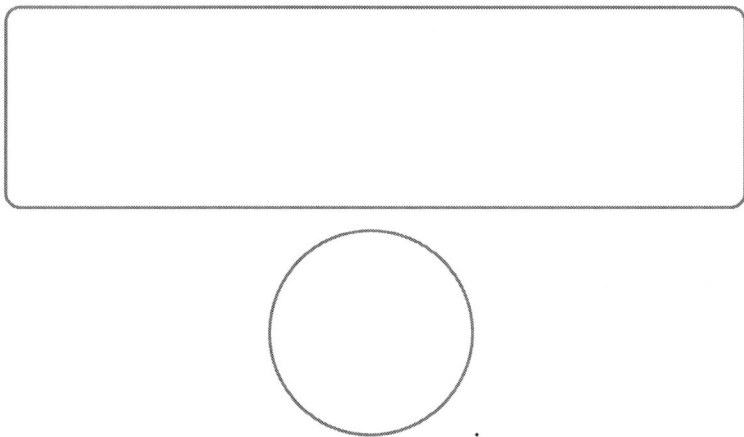

Day 5

Repeat day 1 - 4 in its entirety. Then integrate:

Forgive yourself for any wrong doings known and unknown. Ask God's forgiveness from those you may have offended as soon as possible. Never let the roots of bitterness grow in your garden. You'll spend a life time uprooting them. I wasn't challenged in this area, as I know that there is no condemnation to those who are in Christ and he would forgive me if I forgive them Matthew 6:14.

Lesson learned: forgive quickly, love your self, and relax, breathe deep as often as possible.

Write at least 3 sentences describing your thoughts and feelings in the space below. Then create an image in the circle based on the adjectives described in your rectangle.

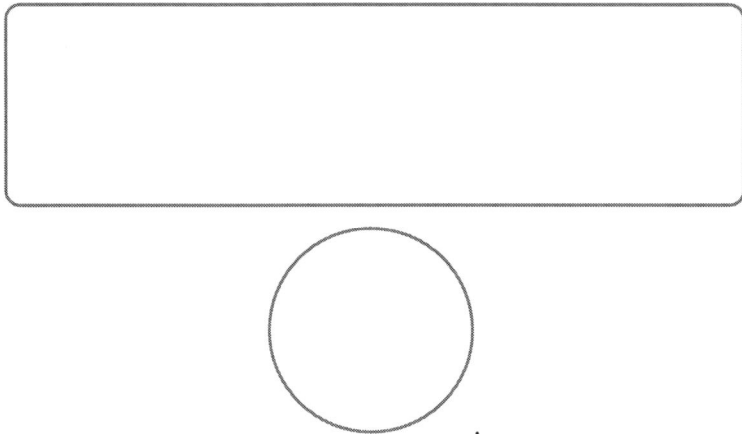

Day 6

Repeat day 1 - 5 in its entirety. Then integrate:

Practice controlling your emotions when wronged, things don't go your way or lack of meeting of the minds with others, Remember, "listening to the Rein" helps reduce stress. Using wisdom and humility always build character too. When I found myself angry while walking, I would notice my feet and back would hurt until I reminded my self of "renewing my mind". My challenge was resetting my thoughts on praiseworthy things and purity of heart.

Lesson learned: not bring things with me during my self-care time, love myself, and let go.

Write at least 3 sentences describing your thoughts and feelings in the rectangle space below. Then create an image in the circle based on the adjectives described in your rectangle.

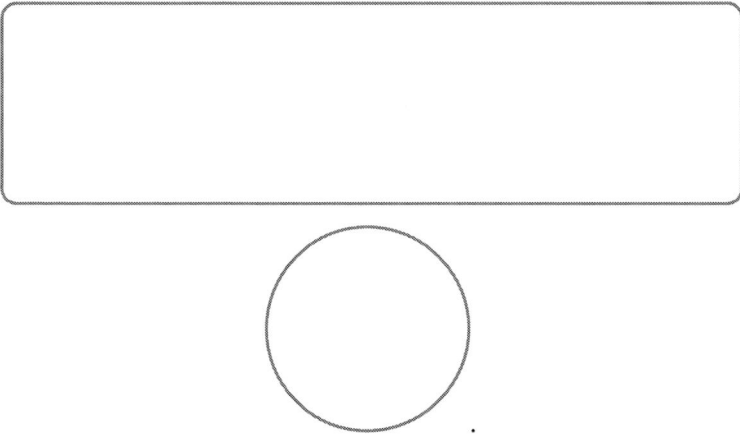

Day 7

Repeat day 1 - 6 in its entirety. Then integrate:

Make a list acknowledging your strengths and weaknesses. This will support knowing who and where you are. As I walked, I immediately reminded myself to forget those things behind me and press forward. Meaning I didn't get hung up on my mistakes and failures.

Lesson learned: that I will strengthen those weak areas just as I build the strong areas. Continue not to judge my thoughts but acknowledge all of them.

Write at least 3 sentences describing your thoughts and feelings in the rectangle space below. Then create an image in the circle based on the adjectives described in your rectangle.

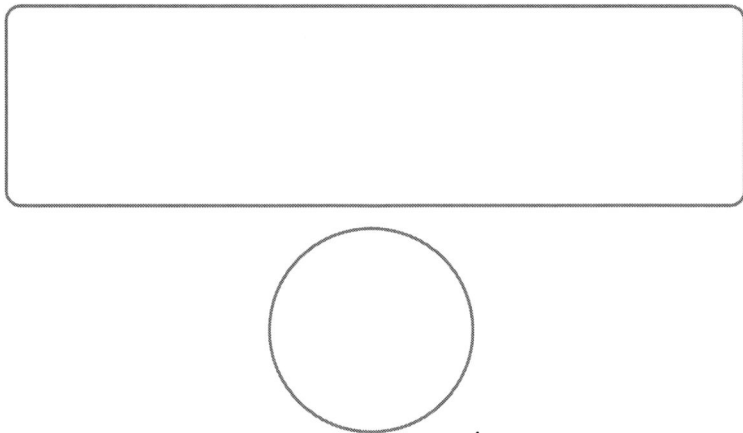

WEEK 1:

DIG DEEP DOWN IN YOUR SOUL for STRENGTH IF YOU ARE DISCOURAGED. AS YOU PRESS FORWARD, SEARCH FOR THE SUNSHINE IN THE REIN!

Day 8

Repeat day 1 - 7 in its entirety. Then integrate:

Notice how you make decisions. Do not make decisions when you feel emotionally and mentally stressed. Many time's I made decisions out of my emotions, however repeating day 1 and 2 helped me to reduce the times I reacted in this way.

Lesson learned: get grounded in who's I am, who I am, and strengthening my inner person.

Write at least 3 sentences describing your thoughts and feelings in the rectangle space below. Then create an image in the circle based on the adjectives described in your rectangle.

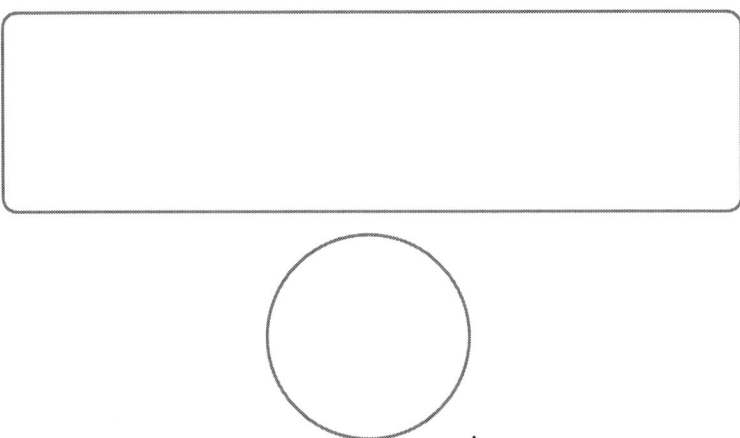

Day 9

Repeat day 1 - 8. Then integrate:

Practice judging all offensive thoughts and hurtful feelings through a "RED" lens. Luke 23:34 then Jesus said, father forgive them; for they know not what they do. Seeing wrongs through God's eyes will help you to see how important it is to let go of negative thoughts and feelings towards protecting your Soul.

Lesson learned: self-love, rest, and peace that passes all understanding.

Write at least 3 sentences describing your thoughts and feelings in the rectangle space below. Then create an image in the circle based on the adjectives described in your rectangle.

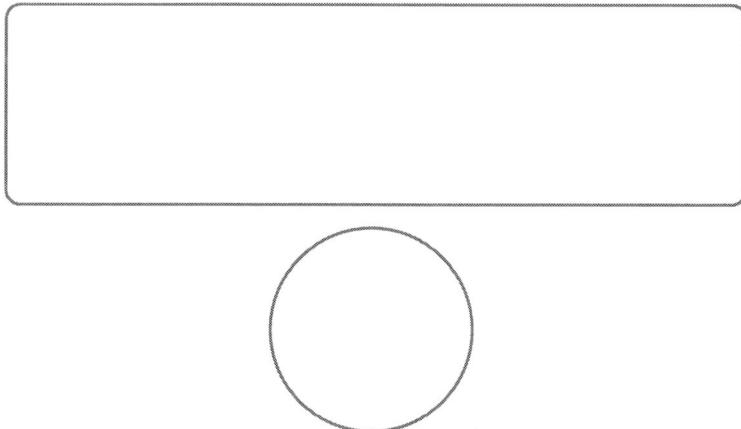

Day 10

Repeat day 1 - 9. Then integrate:

Commit to not listening to music, social media, watching tv, going to movies at least 2 days a month. I noticed I would get too involved with these tools and waist valuable time. Use the time to just be still and be with yourself. This will help you learn the importance of sacrifice and commitment. I noticed I would pick up little annoying phrases and irritating sounds when I was trying to be quiet.

Lesson learned: tune this out more often and self-love.

Write at least 3 sentences describing your thoughts and feelings in the rectangle space below. Then create an image in the circle based on the adjectives described in your rectangle.

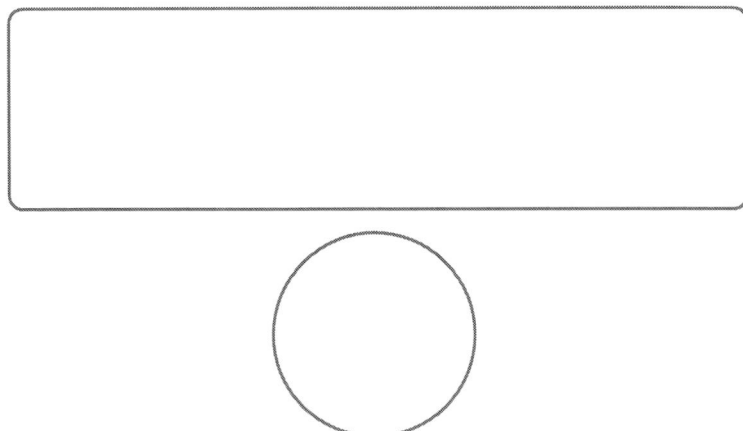

Day 11

Repeat day 1 - 10. Then integrate:

Take a long scenic drive alone (at least 1 hour). Commit to doing at least this 2 times a month. This will support you in renewing your mind in a safe space. It will also support you in hearing clearly the things of God needed for your peace and transformation. I was challenged by letting others dictate my schedule. But I quickly learned missing my drives would cause more stress.

Lesson learned: self-love, quality time with me and newness of strength.

Write at least 3 sentences describing your thoughts and feelings in the rectangle space below. Then create an image in the circle based on the adjectives described in your rectangle.

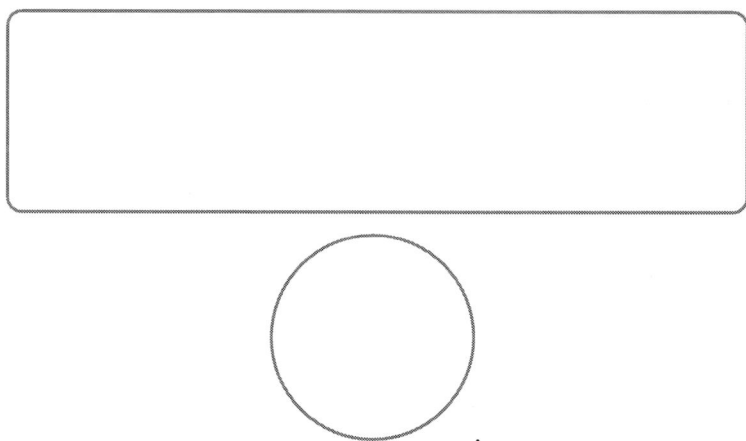

Day 12

Repeat day 1 - 11 in its entirety

Create a HOW YA LUV'N bank using your favorite materials and colors. The bank is used to support positive and productive thoughts and keep you accountable. Also, creating your bank will support your creative process as you notice how you choose each item. As I created my bank I was working hard to make it perfect. However, when I noticed my thoughts and feelings of stress, I released those thoughts.

Lesson learned: stay focused on the process without judgment and relax.

Write at least 3 sentences describing your thoughts and feelings in the rectangle space below. Then create an image in the circle based on the adjectives described in your rectangle.

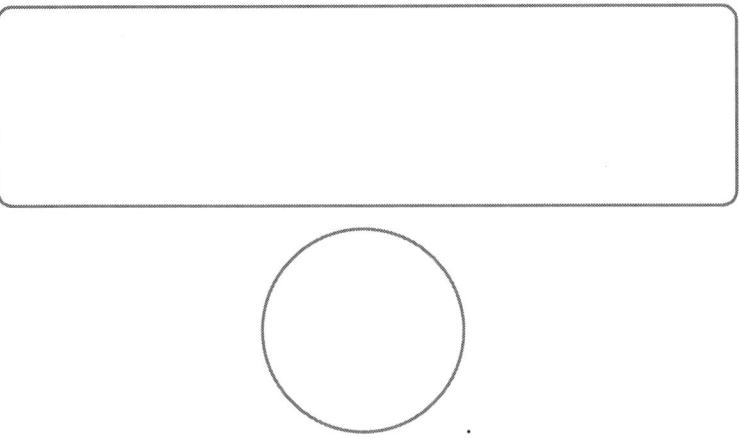

Day 13

Repeat Day 1-12 in its entirety.

Commit to paying $3.00 for every negative unloving thought you have about yourself. At the end of the month, give the money as an offering or to your favorite charity. After counting the cost, it caused me to think more positive of myself and others.

Lesson learned: the process encouraged me to see things from a heart of love and compassion myself. Plus, I was encouraged to truly give what my heart wanted to receive.

Write at least 3 sentences describing your thoughts and feelings in the rectangle space below. Then create an image in the circle based on the adjectives described in your rectangle.

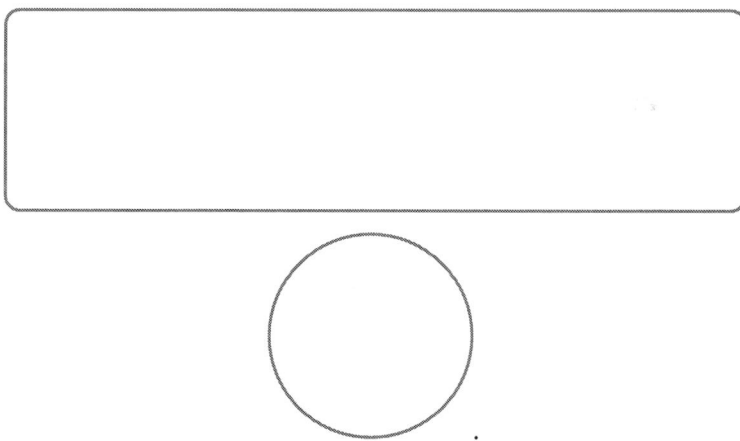

BREATHE!!! YOU MADE IT 14 DAYS! KEEP PRESSING and REFLECT ON WHAT WORKED THESE PAST 2 WEEKS AND CONTINUE IN IT! YOUR BRAIN IS WARMING UP... Transformation should have kicked in.

Day 14

Repeat Day 1-13 in its entirely.

Practice committing to going to a library, grocery store, shopping, carwash, etc outside your immediate community at least 2 times a month. This will allow you to notice how others outside your community support you in HOW YA LUVN - just notice your thoughts.

Lesson learned: see the love of others, trust your intuition, relax, while moving out your comfort zone to enlarge your territory.

Write at least 3 sentences describing your thoughts and feelings in the space below. Then create an image in the circle based on the adjectives described in your rectangle.

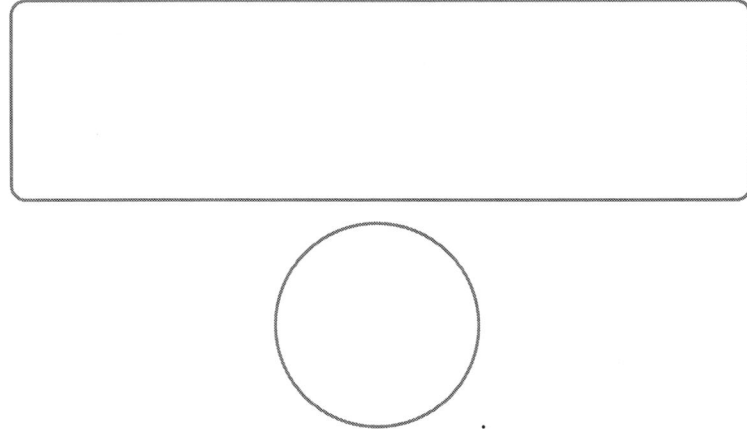

Day 15

Repeat Day 1-14 in its entirety.

Consistently commit to quietly spending at least 30 minutes each day by yourself - no interruptions! This wasn't really a challenge for me as I had been practicing this for years. My challenge was not allowing distractions to come in.

Lesson learned: once I realized the impact on my ability to truly love, I stopped allowing the interruptions.

Write at least 3 sentences describing your thoughts and feelings in the rectangle space below. Then create an image in the circle based on the adjectives described in your rectangle.

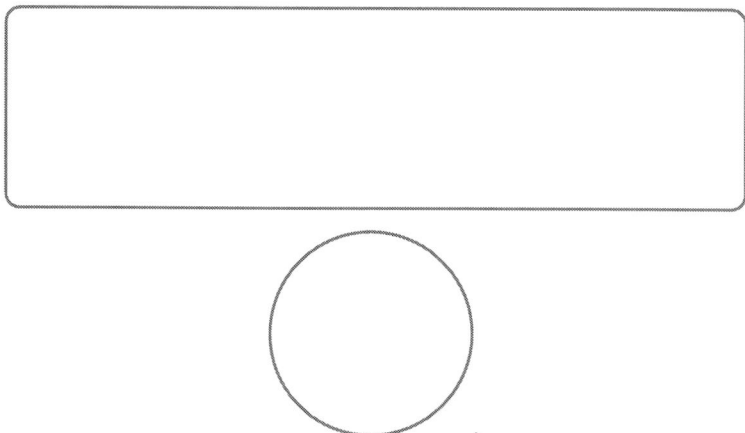

Day 16

Repeat Day 1-15 in its entirety.

Consistently commit to loving your body by thanking and gently massaging each part at the end of the day for supporting you (hands, feet, face, tongue, brain, etc). OMG! This is where the rubber hits the road. If it had not been for these parts I would have collapsed everyday. The work they do and endure daily. Think of your favorite animal and how you care for them. What would happen if they broke down?

Lesson learned: respect and honor my temple through self-love and care daily.

Write at least 3 sentences describing your thoughts and feelings in the rectangle space below. Then create an image in the circle based on the adjectives described in your rectangle.

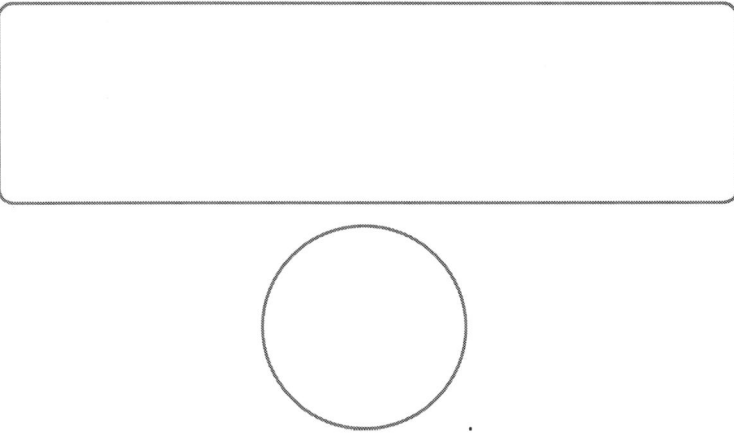

Day 17

Repeat Day 1-16 in its entirety

Commit to taking a soak bath 3 nights a week followed by applying a calming fragrance lotion from head to toe. Soak baths release toxic stress and relaxes the body parts. I felt better emotionally, mentally, and physical after the first week. I threw SHOWERS out the window because it takes too much energy to stand up! Soaks will support a "restful" night sleep.

Lesson learned: make effort to change from routine habits; take necessary time to relax

Write at least 3 sentences describing your thoughts and feelings in the rectangle space below. Then create an image in the circle based on the adjectives described in your rectangle.

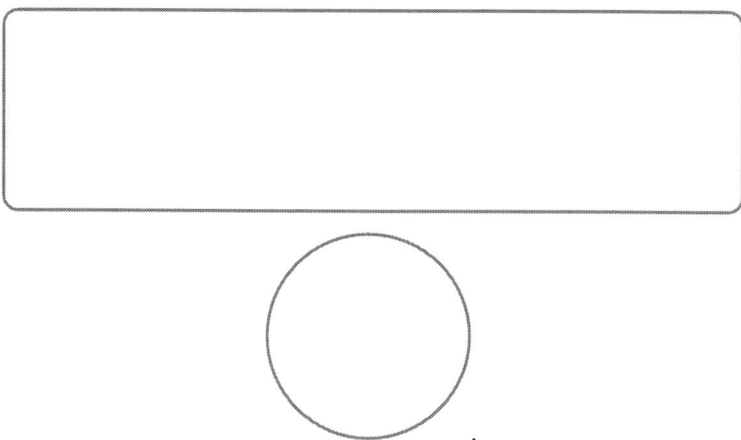

Day 18

Repeat Day 1 - 17 in its entirety.

Commit to self-care at least 2 times a month. Boy, did the thought of getting a massage 2x a month help my psyche in the middle of a busy week. It brought smiles, which relieves stress. Start with your hair and nails and work your way up. See list of benefits for more recommendations.

Lesson learned: self-care does the body and mind good. It doesn't have to cost a lot.

Write at least 3 sentences describing your thoughts and feelings in the rectangle space below. Then create an image in the circle based on the adjectives described in your rectangle.

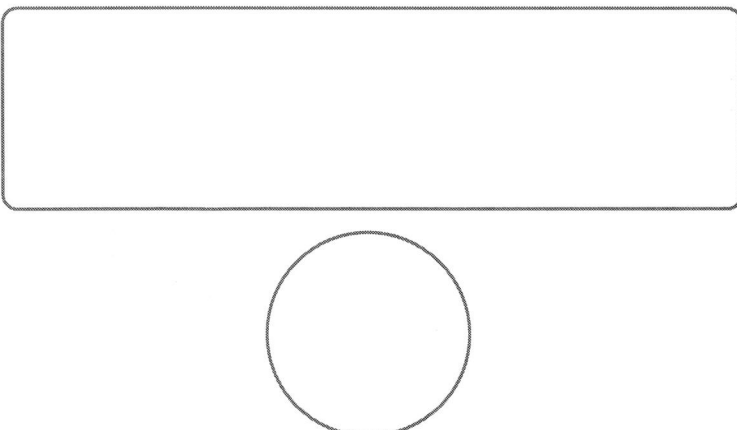

Day 19

Repeat Day 1 - 19 in its entirety.

Commit to drinking at least 3 8oz glasses of water daily for 31 days. This is important as it starts the cleansing process for Spiritual commitment. I started out slow but when I lost a few pounds of toxic liquids and a few inches off the waist, I picked up the pace...great physical support.

Lesson learned: drink, drink to avoid mental and physical dehydration.

Write at least 3 sentences describing your thoughts and feelings in the rectangle space below. Then create an image in the circle based on the adjectives described in your rectangle.

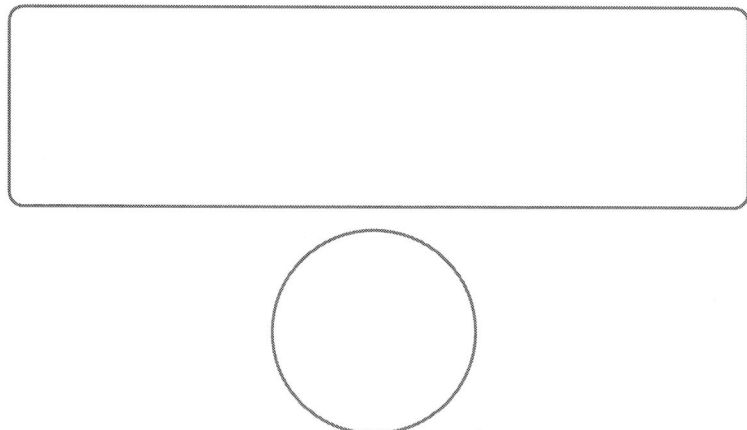

Day 20

Repeat Day 1 - 19 in its entirety.

Commit to not eating after 7pm Monday-Saturday for 31 days. Yikes, easy weezy the first and second day, but when you're burning late hours it can be a challenge. I noticed I became sleepy earlier than usual. Naw, cut back on the food.

Lesson learned: how to have staying power (endurance) on the way to building spiritual commitment.

Write at least 3 sentences describing your thoughts and feelings in the rectangle space below. Then create an image in the circle based on the adjectives described in your rectangle.

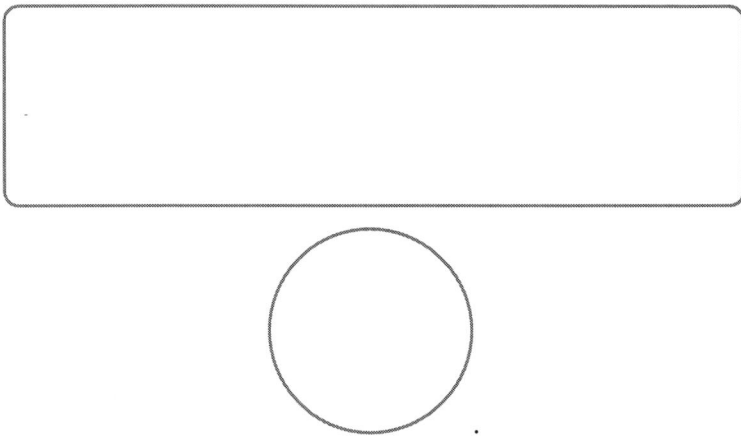

Day 21

Repeat Day 1 - 20 in its entirety.

Commit to saying "NO" to sugared foods and drinks weekly (as much as possible). This drug was my worst nightmare! He drug me down fast until wonder woman came to the scene and reminded me of the work to be done. I'm still challenged but not as much.

Lesson learned: my overall health and LUV'N myself improved might I say quickly! Yours can too.

Write at least 3 sentences describing your thoughts and feelings in the rectangle space below. Then create an image in the circle based on the adjectives described in your rectangle.

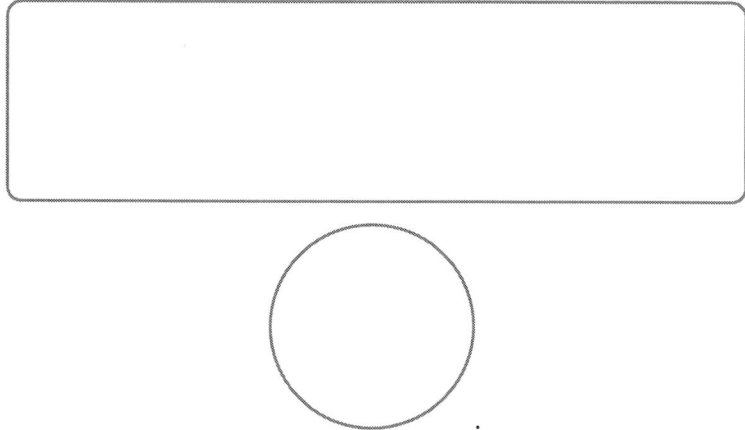

Day 22

Repeat Day 1 - 21 in its entirety.

Commit to creating a safe space at home and work to be mindful. Commit to entering that space at least 3 times a day. This will support a truly authentic relationship with YOU as much as it will with God.

Lesson learned: creating and having a special "safe space" to go will encourage you to be mindful often.

Write at least 3 sentences describing your thoughts and feelings in the rectangle space below. Then create an image in the circle based on the adjectives described in your rectangle.

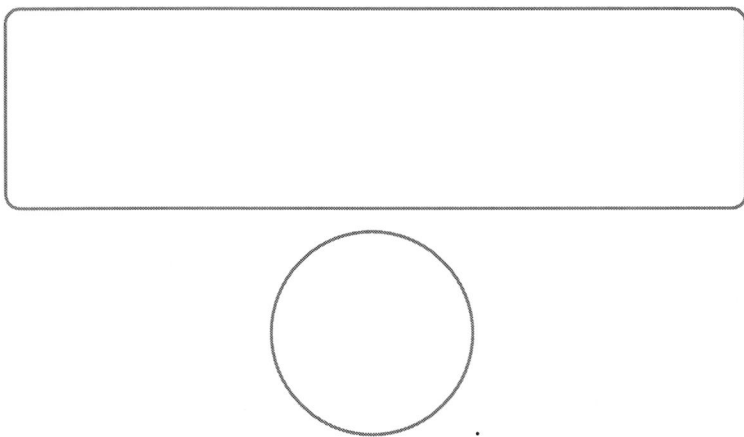

Day 23

Repeat Day 1 - 22 in its entirety.

Commit to telling yourself "NO" to watching sitcoms and drama series (Scandal, Empire, Have and Have Nots, movies, etc) or any TV, video, youtube, tapes, audio productions that has a perverted truth! I was guilty with Greenleaf and Queen Sugar. Great shows until it turned into a soap. While this is reality on so many levels, I still didn't want to promote the underlining message (hurt and pain).

Lesson learned: guarding my eyes, ears, and heart that distract true authentic love. Practice makes perfect!

Write at least 3 sentences describing your thoughts and feelings in the rectangle space below. Then create an image in the circle based on the adjectives described in your rectangle.

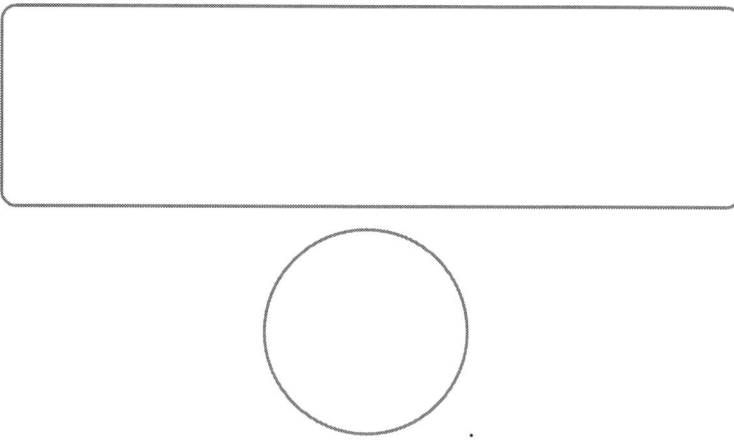

Day 24

Repeat Day 1 - 23 in its entirety.

Commit to reading a Proverb each day for 31 days, Repeat monthly. Knowledge is power and you will need it more once you're LUV'N more authentically. It saved my life many days when I first started out, as I had just read something and it would unfold right before my eyes.

Lesson learned: Solomon gave the instructions, but didn't always adhere to it. However, I can learn from his mistakes.

Write at least 3 sentences describing your thoughts and feelings in the rectangle space below. Then create an image in the circle based on the adjectives described in your rectangle.

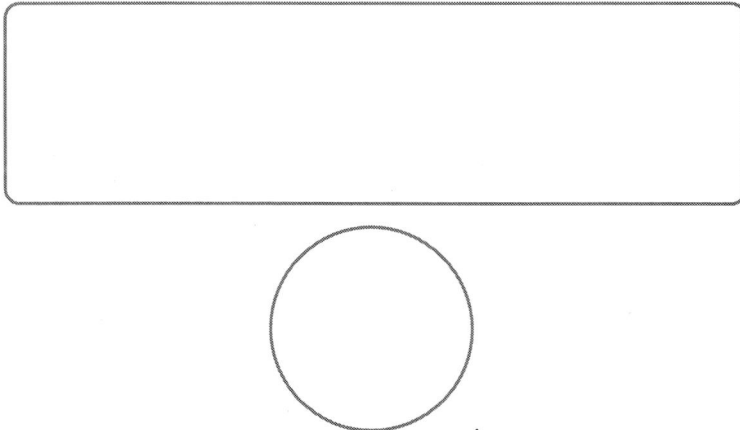

Day 25

Repeat Day 1 - 24 in its entirety.

Commit to living faithful, honest, generous, and open hearted. Also commit to addressing the issues of your heart daily (anger, hatred, jealousy, hurt etc). I thought I had fully released my anger against someone who hurt me, but it was revealed as I started being more open hearted.

Lesson learned: acknowledge, accept, and trust my feelings to get my truth.

Write at least 3 sentences describing your thoughts and feelings in the rectangle space below. Then create an image in the circle based on the adjectives described in your rectangle.

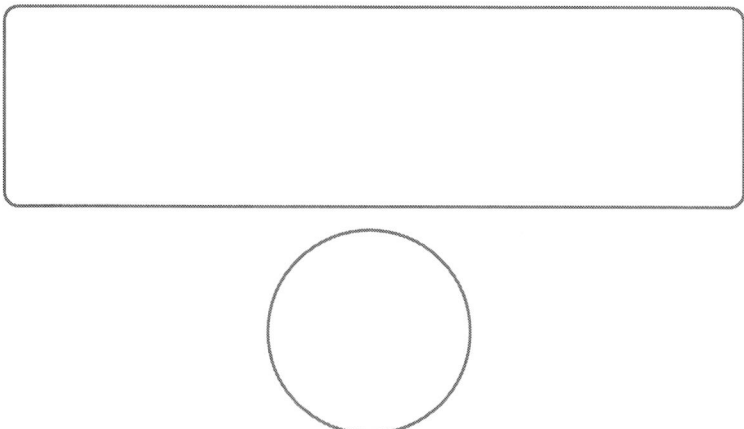

Day 26

Repeat Day 1 - 25 in its entirety.

Commit daily not to respond or participate in negative or gossip conversations. Consistently commit to covering the wrongs of others. This will build character and integrity (influencer). Do this especially for those that have hurt you!

Lesson learned: set free as a bird, now I can soar! Proverb 17:9 states he who covers a transgression seeks LOVE.

Write at least 3 sentences describing your thoughts and feelings in the rectangle space below. Then create an image in the circle based on the adjectives described in your rectangle.

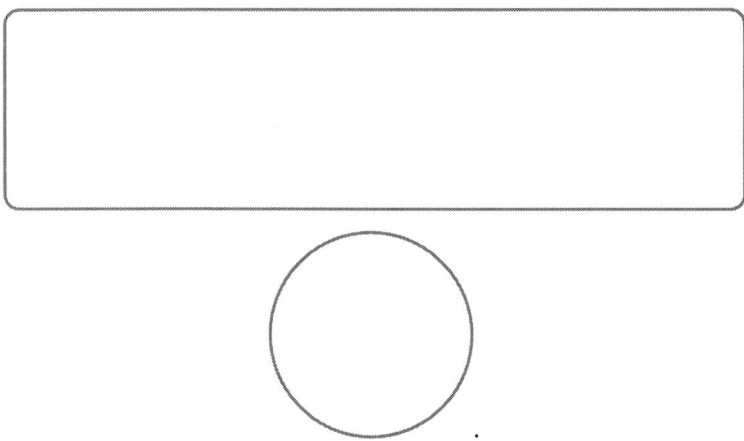

Day 27

Repeat Day 1 - 26 in its entirety.

Commit to telling yourself "NO" when tempted to over spend, over eat, over stay, or over do. (Impulsive actions create a lack of self-control). I struggled with over eating when working on projects. It seemed to keep me busy until my health started to fail. NO, became easier while gaining self- control and LUV'N me.

Lesson learned: say NO more often it won't hurt!

Write at least 3 sentences describing your thoughts and feelings in the rectangle space below. Then create an image in the circle based on the adjectives described in your rectangle.

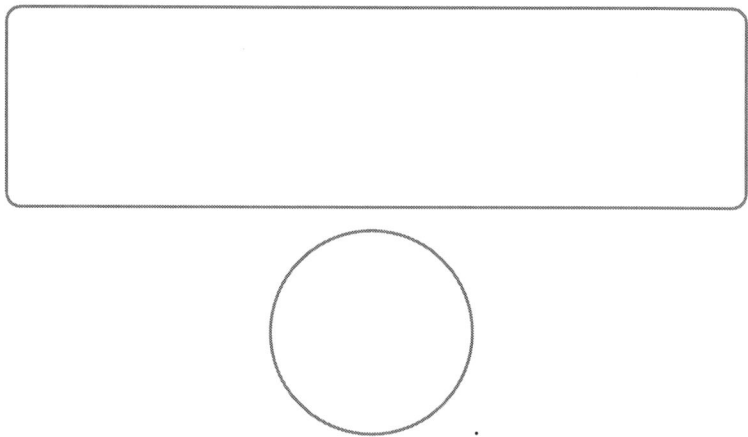

Day 28

Repeat Day 1 - 27 in its entirety.

Commit to not talking on the phone after 10pm for 31 days. This cuts down on the voices in your head before bed time. I was challenged with this for a minute as I have family that only called at night due to work schedules. However, when I started having certain dreams about conversation with them it was time to shut it down. Proverb 3:24, tells us we are to have sweet sleep.

Lesson learned: limit late night conversations as much as possible.

Write at least 3 sentences describing your thoughts and feelings in the rectangle space below. Then create an image in the circle based on the adjectives described in your rectangle.

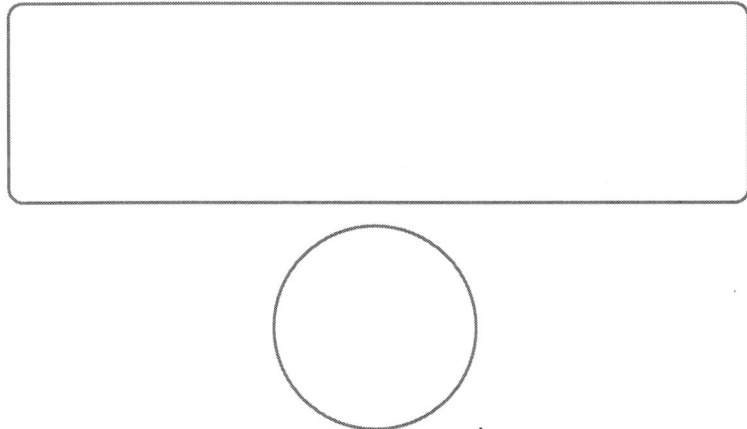

Day 29

Repeat Day 1 - 28 in its entirety.

Commit to smiling at everyone as you make a nice compliment daily. Thank God for this because the other person didn't know it was helping me more than them. What I gave to them, I had to first learn to give to myself.

Lesson learned: no longer passed me by, self-love.

Write at least 3 sentences describing your thoughts and feelings in the rectangle space below. Then create an image in the circle based on the adjectives described in your rectangle.

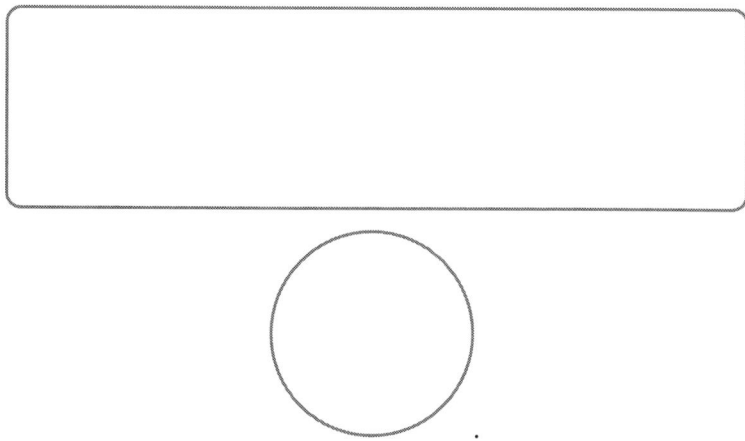

Day 30

Repeat Day 1 - 29 in its entirely.

Commit to journaling your progress daily, if not weekly. I did this daily to record my thoughts and feelings - good and bad, happy or sad, up and down, spiritually and naturally. I wanted to reflect on things to see where I was going. Divine intervention is worth recording.

Lesson learned: commit to journaling at least 1x a day.

Write at least 3 sentences describing your thoughts and feelings in the rectangle space below. Then create an image in the circle based on the adjectives described in your rectangle.

CONGRATULATIONS! You made it! I pray you reward yourself with something very special!

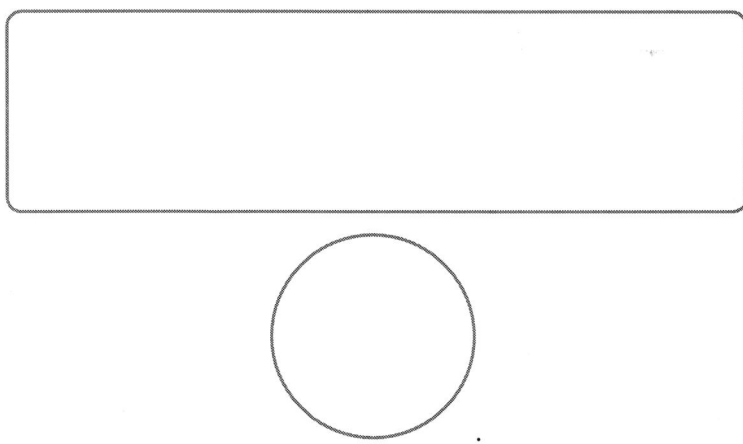

Day 31

Repeat Day 1 - 30 in its entirety.

Consistently commit to LUV'N yourself daily by praying, trusting your voice, and repeat this journal at least 3 consecutive times or until you master as many days as possible. Don't give up when you don't accomplish a day or two but spend more time being mindful to strengthen your commitment. Enjoy the journey as you start LUV'N you more!

Lesson learned: self-care, self-love, moment by moment listening and trusting your voice.

Write at least 3 sentences describing your thoughts and feelings in the rectangle space below. Then create an image in the circle based on the adjectives described in your rectangle.

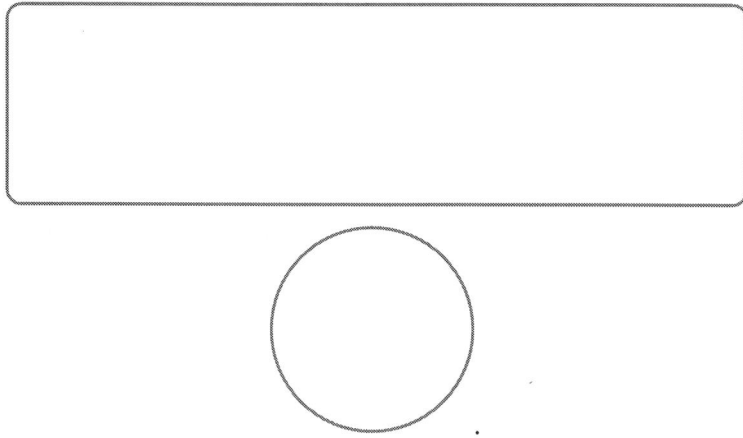

BENEFITS

The benefits to being Mindful (renewing) have helped many people to transform into wise and loving hearted individuals. Self-care through mindfulness allows you to learn how to transform the way you feel, think, work, and love. Practicing mindfulness, even for just 8 weeks, can bring a myriad of physical, psychological, and social benefits. Some of the benefits are but not limited to:

- improve positive emotions

- pay attention more, memory

- reduce stress and decrease depression

- changes the brain to improve emotion regulation, empathy

- foster compassion and altruism,

- self-awareness and compassion

- weight reduction

- reduces behavior problems and aggression,

- enhances relationships - more optimistic, accepting of others

Suggested activities to support your journey to consistently LUV'N YOU:

MIND: daily mindfulness, calm and relaxing meditation music, reading and using the SENS'RE 3 Rein Stick at least 8 minutes a day, 5 days a week.

BODY: massage at least 2x a month, manicure/pedicure, desired exercise, ***nature walks**, dancing, deep breathing to release stress, reflexology, *self massage, *walk in clinics (student interns), *community centers, church health expos, *medical and health conventions, etc.

*low cost to free services.

SPIRIT: reading the scriptures daily, Art making, using the Rein Stick, listen to meditation music, guided meditations, solitude practices.

Suggested bath products:

Aromatherapy Bath products:

- Eucalyptus Spearmint

- Lavender vanilla

- Lavender chamomile

- Sandlewood, sage, or lemongrass fragrance

- Calming music

- Exfoliating bath gloves

- Long handle - Bath Brush

- Candles: eucalyptus, sandlewood, sage, lavender, vanilla, linen

- Cotton towels, slippers, bathrobe

- Bed Linen spray

MINDFUL CROSSWORD PUZZLE: MINDFULLNESS IS: file:///
Users / pamelalittle / Documents /
how%20ya%20luvn%20puzzle.webarchive

About the Author

Ms. Little is a Licensed Clinical Professional Counselor, Art and Registered Play Therapist with over 15 years of experience helping children, adolescents and their families. In 2013, out of her passion to help others find their "true value" in life she founded SENS'RE 3 Coaching and Consulting, LLC. As she focused on removing the obstacles that stood between her client and emotional self-control, the SENS'RE 3 Mindfulness tool was birthed. The SENS'RE 3 Rein Stick® promotes peace and harmony to mind, body, and spirit.

Ms. Little serves in ministry and graduated Master Life Discipleship training in 2016.

CALLED TO SERVE

Call today to join the SENS'RE 3 Academy. This eight-week coaching program teaches you how to integrate mindfulness and art into your life to reduce anxiety, depression, and other mental health symptoms. When you call and join, you will receive a free "HOW YA LUV'N" heart magnet.

Please visit www.sensre3.com to contact Ms. Little to set up a complimentary, no obligation, 30-minute discovery call to see how we can continue to transform your personal lifestyle. Also you can request her for speaking engagements and bulk orders.

Made in the USA
Middletown, DE
24 November 2021

53205189R00029